For Lack of a Dictionary

For Lack
of a
Dictionary

Poems

Rosalind Morris

Fordham University Press   New York   2025

Fordham University Press has no responsibility for the persistence or accuracy of URLs for external or third-party Internet websites referred to in this publication and does not guarantee that any content on such websites is, or will remain, accurate or appropriate.

Fordham University Press also publishes its books in a variety of electronic formats. Some content that appears in print may not be available in electronic books.

Visit us online at www.fordhampress.com.

For EU safety / GPSR concerns:
Mare Nostrum Group B.V.
Mauritskade 21D
1091 GC Amsterdam, The Netherlands
gpsr@mare-nostrum.co.uk

Printed in the United States of America

25 24 23   5 4 3 2 1

First edition

for Yvette

Contents

Something Gets Planted

For Lack of a Dictionary

If I Am

If I Am Six

If I am six years old
I know the days are longest in summer,
that night expands in winter
like ink on wet paper, that darkness leaks
and is said to contain evil.

At six years old, the relativity of time consists
in summer's latelight, the long tri-tone song of crickets.

If I am six years old, the bull rushes are measured
by me. I know the blue heron has two legs, but not
that two dragonflies, attached and arched
in awkward flight, are suffering a need
which I have not yet called desire,
only that flight is dangerous at the best of times.

A mosquito whines and stops whining.
I have learned to wait for this absence of sound
before slapping.

If I am six years old, I wait
in patience
attend the dark and dewcool,
listen for the sound of leaf unfurling, the stalk bending,
eyelashes brushing against each other as my heart thuds
like the windshield wipers on Daddy's car.

Already I know the pleasure of survival, the thrill
of lasting longer than everything else.

Now: in the greenlight,
above still water,

a movement:
leaf descending, stem arching as though to break.
The tree frog
launches itself horizontal
and my hand stabs the air.

Even before beginning its descent
in hunger
my hand
    flung like a bullet
finds its mark, clasps desperately

not knowing that clasping is a gesture

of desire
or affection
or grief,
as when a lover has left
or a child has died, unfairly.

Awful this sensation: heart of another beating
in my own hand, tiny but sharp, striking palm
as though my flesh enclosed it, was second skin,
my hand a cage of ribs.
Horrible too, this cessation,
this breaking of a heart
in my own hand

and the quiet of it.

If I Am Seven

If I am seven years old
my father and I are sitting
on the balcony,
closest to roof-top without danger,
and I am under his great arm
following the finger not broken
to the loyalist star in the universe —
Sirius: at the heel, under sword.

This is the place where
            once (then)
ancient people mapped themselves
ideal, and found familiars
to stave off the humiliation
of a sky unresponsive
and so much larger than any empire.

My father tells me that light comes
from afar and takes time to arrive.

How long?
            Very long.
How long is very long?
            Many millions of years.
How long is that?
            Almost forever.

If it takes so long then we too
shall be dead when perceived,
like God, showing himself from behind
and Moses glimpsing just the trace
of his passing (such disappointment!).

This is more than I can bear

if I am seven years old.

But it hurts, like tonsils, from deep inside,
makes breathing hard and fast,
renders speech a kind of ache.

Ten in the Library

I find my name among them:
Rosalind feigning love of women,
photographing a double helix,
playing the ham in Hollywood.

There are others, I think.
I will become one.

Eleven: Grammar Lessons

Absolute infinitive: to be tested.
Write an essay about the history of flight.
The librarian gives me a book about
Amelia Earhart. Her lack of fear
of loneliness
frightens me.
One and one more. Too many times across the sea.

We gather seeds and learn that even
trees reproduce sexually. I run home
to explain what it means
to blaze and not be consumed.

At eleven, symbiosis is the most difficult word
I can spell.

In April, I dream of summer:
batwing and mosquito,
the sound of teenagers throbbing
under lamplight.
I walk to the seaside,
observe the boys take their early boats to sea,
watch the osprey circling.

One and one. Clouds accumulate.
It is a year of unseasonal storms.

South of us, on Highway 1,
past the redwoods,
beyond the mossy root,
greenmist and barking sealion coasts,

it must be sunny.

Befindlichkeit

By eleven, I know how
the columns accumulate
        without adding up.
One and one. Not two but one more.
I have learned the infinitive form
of every verb for 'to feel.'

One year in, I am still the new girl
in the new school.

Under the periodic table,
between the H's,
        his and hers,
boys and new breasts sit in neat rows
like kennel dogs
sniffing for weakness.

I cover my scent with indifference,
ask for new shoes and bluejeans,
and watch the osprey careening
in cloudstorms above the gravel yard
where the oldest boys
make smoke rings, snort obscenities.

Our classroom: a sanctum of vinyl chairs
and linoleum squares
under the Queen's grey gaze.

In the library, famous women
go to war,
preside over empires
and die mysteriously,
        smelling of printer's ink.

The teacher smells of chalk and coffee,
praises my handwriting,
       approves my reading skills.

I admire the barren Curie
and experiment with flies.

The New Girl

Because I am the new girl in the new school
who dreams of radium
(with flies in her hair)
they choose me to make the tea
when the prettiest among us
stays home, her
brothers being lost at sea.

Unseen by magazine gods
the pretty ones sob, by grief
possessed. Tears and sighs
ebb and flow with the
arrival of each teacher.

Outside, the bells of the normal day
ring, echo in the halls.
The cedars sway,
boys and new breasts
fight under the tether-ball.

Because I am the new girl
at the new school
I pour the brew
(too weak and then too strong)
in grateful sympathy.

Salt fills the room
crusts each in shameless turn,
rims our cups
and clouds the air,
a mournful scene

where neither the school
nor I any longer are new.

Amid deodorant pine and
banana loaf, Red Roses and
stale carnations: the smell
of kelp, fetid weed of the
ebbing sea.

I do not ask about those brothers,
open-mouthed in water
or on the foam-traced shore,
amid the buoys and beer bottles
and the moaning gulls, doubling

unlicensed grief of the once-new girl.

Outside, ospreys
plough the sky,
robin and song-sparrow
flit across the grass, hide in shrubs.

We learn to identify birds
by their songs, but I know already
the cracksplatter of shell
on rock beneath the raptor's wing,
the shwip of talon at wavebreak
when needy fish come to the surface.

Patty Hearst Pays a Visit

A pretty girl with long dark hair
and magazine looks is on television,
holding a gun in a bank.

Eleven charges.
One and one.

Were we warborn?
Unfold the sequence, one after one.

This is the beginning of the sequence:
I will. I can.
Can I, a girl?

Everyone Burns Their Witches

Fear and I Are Twins

after Thomas Hobbes, for Tony

In the future, after the lilacs
and the last grey gunshot,
when the prayers of desperate
men have returned their echo
and arbors have reclaimed the pavement

everything will be fragment.

Will they know us (?) you ask,
headache in hands (behind closed doors
there is rancid milk and falling hair).

> All that we know, he says, is material:
> a stone-strewn street in Malmesbury,
> rain unrhythmic, nightsoil mingled with honeysuckle.
> But the seed of sow-thistle from the Thames' marauding
>
> edge, dragged hither beneath a coalboy's shoe,
> spreads yellow where grey had dominion, and mocks
> the will to order.

Will they read the signs we make
to mark our passing? Cigarette butts
and chewing gum, and in the desert,
our corpses adorned by plastic bottles.

> He says: *The register of knowledge of fact
> is called history.*

Who, us? Who to know?
How to find the way when
neither lilac nor gunshot
nor prayerful men to lead the way?

Much memory, or the memory of many things
is called experience.

He bends, adjusting buckle and bow,
ash in the fold of old linen. His neck
is greased by an unclean sky and
one cuff has dredged the soup bowl's lip.

We are librarians who inhabit
a fluorescent dark, recall what
others knew, by fragment and scent
of fear.

In all places, where men have lived by small families,
to rob and spoil each other has been a trade.

So, *fear and desire alike will have their objects.*

An archive of rumors
hums in the whiteknuckled night.

He touches his sovereigns for comfort,
shops for cheap pepper in a time of war.

You say everything
could have been forgiven
if forgotten.

The first law of economics is vengeance.

Sweet discovery: who pressed
old flowers between dry leaves,
to mark the place of word or bone?

He lets no ceremony of ghosts
waste frankincense or myrrh.

The passages on war have dog-ears,
thumb-prints in the margins. And where
a kiss, the page is thin. Mark
the spot of desire with use.
Then will they know us.

He says: *The reputation of power, is power.*

And fear, you ask,
what is its trace?

He locks the doors twice, hides his coins,
paints red the sign of the cross. Clarion the call
from beneath his shuttered door:
Burn the dead, confine the poor,
appoint the rat a king.

The passages on money are noted
in a ledger at the end of every book.

Rhume and tremor, he addresses the glass man
of echoes: Fear, my twin, if not a sovereign,
then plague, and war, and fire.
To presence or absence assign
a head.

Above us, the last bird breaking song
throws shadow on a ruined tracery of road and
bridge and somewhere, to sea, a new island
glints artificially. What pattern survives us
grows there, at the limit. Yes, you say, we
have raised our flag above it.

As for witches, I think not that
their witchcraft is any real power, but yet they are justly
punished, for the false belief they have.

In the desert, we build
a bonfire of the largest books.

       Short of ink and sealing wax,
       he falls prey to an ever-incandescing suspicion
       of human order:
       Everyone burns their witches.

The smoke that chars us
rises unseen and undeciphered,
falls blackly to earth and pocks
the land with acid.

Huntsville, TX

homage to Adrienne Rich

1.

At first, we knew the time of execution
by the clock which, ticking sternly,
rose to the perpendicular
and cut the world away.

Then, we knew by the falter in light bulbs,
the shudder of night that shook the room
above bridge tables and coffee pots,
startling conversation.
                        We knew
when, after brief spasms, darkness
returned to the world behind windows
and the lamplight steadied.

In small towns
there was never enough current
for both electrocution
and more than one lamp
in the kitchen.

2.

Sibilant
         this last sigh,
rushing across the burnt fields
of a broken republic
         where corn once grew,

sibilant
         this last sigh

rushing forth like wind,
elemental   like spite

sibilant,   this consummate breath
of the righteous.

     Whereas
   three black men were, in the year
   nineteen hundred and twenty-three,
   burned alive at the stake
   in the county of ....
   before an audience of approximately ...
   and without trial, nor the appearance of justice,
   the State of Texas decrees an end
   to spectacular deaths.

Let us then clasp
the guilty in secret embrace,

     for we are just.

Sibilant
   this last exhalation
in which the people relieve themselves
and enter quietly the communion
of executioners, muttering,
muttering to themselves
muttering:

   at last

   at last   at last.

3.

Atlas of a ravaged land, these
splayed pages of desolation
are crossed a thousand times by rage
         and more by fear.

It takes a cartographer
to find here a single path
amid the tangled lines
which mark   not space
but the hot flow of white energy

         and hate

but also jealousy.

4.

Icarus sits in a halo of flicking light and
observes two points of a compass
then draws an arc
from which a new sun hangs.

Is this the point of relative inaccessibility?

Two points of a compass: the first point
illumination, the second point shadow.

5.

Every witness will tell you

         the same thing.

What you notice first

             and last

is the way the upper lip curls back
to reveal, better than any dissection,
the way the teeth hang like droplets
from gums (which are purple
at the roots and glistening).

What you notice first

             and last

is the way the mouth gapes, the way
the face opens, the way it splays itself:
ashamed,
unredeemed by laughter.

There is no second impression —

only that curl of lip, suddenly canine
(and the humiliation of this), only the strain
of wrists against the leather cuff,
the mass of torso pulling away
from the hard back of the chair
(the chair like any other), only
the moaning chafe of the brace
pressing again on the ankle, only
the bare feet gripping the cold floor,
the beads of sweat forming along
the forehead, at the hairline,
in the small concave between clavicles,
only the hands closing around the arms
of the chair, only the evaporation of steam
in small sighs from shaven flesh,
only the smell of piss leaking into the room

and the improbable recollection of pork
that this smoke calls forth,
only the longing for relief
from that groaning current
that buzzes the air and conducts itself
through the shining metal
still lodged in naked teeth.

6.

Tonight, at midnight, sixteen days
since the last death, the chair
will shine briefly in a moonlight
interrupted only by moths.

And there will be a clenching
before witnesses.

In the antechamber, behind a grey curtain,
journalists and others who have endured
months on waiting lists
will attend their reward.

Six weeks. Eight months. This is my first.

7.

Last requests: the pathos of ice cream,
hamburgers, unfiltered cigarettes…
                    (is beer allowed?)

None denied but labor.   And time.

This last labor denied,
hardest heroism, meanest decision:

```
not to try          again    to breathe
to not try          again    to breathe
```

I would have had this last sovereignty:
to refuse desperation. And
it would almost have been enough.

But this vengeance against fear
is — at last — surrender. I am yours
as much as any lover.

So: a gift: I give you this satisfaction
(oh, you pretty boys with your football jackets).
You win. Or at least I will have lost more.

I could think of other deaths,
easier perhaps, or maybe just neater,
no burning, no stiffening
                (is this the limit of mercy?)

but also worse. Floating gaseous
behind glass,
                like a fish exiled to air.

If you looked closely, met my gaze,
you would see Lake Michigan, ice heaving upward,
deforming the shore from behind my eyes.

But this is not a last request. There are
other things more pressing. In the end
a cliché: everything is a question of timing.

So, if this last labor be taken from me
by unnatural fire, then
please
                let it be in winter.

If in a Tomb

*…you shall know, my sons, shall know
why we leave the song unsung*
—Ethel Rosenberg, *"If We Die"*

Ethel to Julius.

I.

How long can I wait to pay the bills

if in a tomb
        I am sealed?

The accountant will be in next week

It took them just a few days to realize I could sing

(except for the matron)

I am knitting a lovely green sweater

They'll be putting the lights out soon
— only this means of communication

There is for me a sense of taking hold,
coming to grips with hard circumstance

If a real cure could be effected:

unbelievable,
       unthinkable,
       heart-stopping,
but
     all in vain

I need you so to be strong for me

I am knitting a lovely green sweater

Honey, let's go home

2.

frenzied longing I must deny

…reluctant my step

monotonous days
       held fast by brick

Shall our love put forth gripping root?

Here shall we roar defiance

Your lonely wife
a fine intermittent rain

Disconsolately:
       the few green things pushing their way up
       the leaves of a wild plant unfold
almost hiding two buds

…in this crevice an apple seed

It is because we didn't hesitate

Blazon forth those answers
       within the walls of Sing Sing
       until the truth…

(a wise man, whose name I forget)

It is torture:
we may never be with them again

I never was so much in love

My own legal murder

No pasaran!

Hold me close

No pasaran!

My own legal murder

...in this crevice an apple seed.

3.

Here is what I have been dreaming
I'm putting it in the form of a monologue:

A car could strike

The words are probably not—
even imperfectly...
enough

(!) Answer briefly that it is painless

Let's not be afraid

Nor can I, needless to say, escape the terrible ache

Where is there an end?

If by your silence you permit this deed...

Good night, with all my heart

I have a curious feeling of living
        toward which I tend
        in a world beyond whose walls
        no other world exists

I have yet to dream
        less strangeness and terror

This blue and golden day
        closed my eyes:
it was a forgetfulness
        I sought desperately
with grief in my mind's eye
not to be imagined.

The children haunt me

Between now and...
Now I am thirty-six years old

The darkened streets
meaningless gesture

Winter
        Preliminary
        Lowering sky

Scorning

The wind's sharp sting

If Monday comes…

The thought of you warm
        unspeakable sweet within me

the Shofar sounding
such intense hunger…

A wave of wanting washes —

(the rain prompted me to quote)

He is so young, so young

Between hilarity and depression
        I get so hopeful

I have done all the crying

Tonight
it is Monday morning

Where is that magic formula
        that will insure
          our happy ending?

…a car could strike

4.

The storm is spent

this lonely visitless weekend

Determinedly through the snow
a cold fury possesses me

(Courage, darling, there's much to be done:
the need to maintain a genuine cheerfulness)

If only we could be together

I could eat you in sheer extremity of feeling

A fairly presentable woman
so impossibly lonely...

I am lashed

You madden yourself with words:
so many burned-out stars
            all, all past

Essentially, it is a simple decision:
            Commit new errors,
            Monster, grow stronger

I, while awaiting execution

even if clemency is denied

I shall live

            die without dying

A cold fury possesses me

a Sepulchre in which I shall

madden   live   die.

Julius to Ethel

Aside from the fact that we are innocent…
A chicken dinner reminds me that it is thanksgiving.

Letter to the Front in a Time of AIDS

…only the women and poets know
—Muriel Rukeyser

1.

First: the desperate beauty of the paper
unadorned, the naked waiting for the cut,
for the ink, for the word   *dearest*

And then the weather: clear skies or storms,
an unusual harvest of peaches, and the sounds
of summer cicadas and mothwing thunder

under new lamplight. Expenses made
come next of course, and the catalogue of things
still to buy but not yet needed, and things

that can be made or mended at home, now that
there is so little to do but wait   and attend
balls where the women dance breast to breast

and toothless men or legless boys sit, propped
against the wall, leaving sweat-stains on old brick
and piss-stink on the wall behind the church.

Only women and poets   dancing
breast to breast   while the children sleep.

2.

And what shall we do now? To whom
address the word, dearest? For whom this cut
be borne? For what endure the needful eyes

of those who long for war
when there is no front, just this moving line,
circling, invading, cutting into halves

like peaches, our lives, our fingers stuck by pins
and nothing holding together, not even
the line, just this movement, this sense

that moving might keep us safe and
not knowing, not knowing from what
we move but going anyway   to the fields

where the harvest waits. Already dead
our boys, this awful growing of their open eyes,
and the women poets, dancing

and wanting to say, wanting to hear, learning to say
dearest, dearest, while dancing breast to breast.

Late Night News

Who sends the sun sublimely
to death? A mother cries next

to a hollow bus & men are busy
in the rhythm of flashing lights.

Who sends the son sublimely
to death? School books are shucked

for dynamite and burnt wings.

Another mother cries in a hollow room
unlit by electric light, to see

for the last time, a boy, a girl,
a skipping rope that is not yet

a noose. Who sends the son?
Sublimely to death he goes, and so

he arrives, without thought or wings.

Cinders flutter above
the hollow dream, and a blue line travels

to the moon in search of a flag on
unclaimed land. Who sends, to death,

the son? Another mother cries, illiterate
in grief, but learning quickly the sounds

of soon-familiar words: too soon   too late.

Here and There

Here: grey sky and greying still
(steel, not silver, on the horizon)
mouths metallic, tin on the tongue
and words clanging in streets
where the last protester has left coffee
cups and footprints in yesterday's snow.

There: hard to say, a cold day,
might be clear.

We imagine here as there: houses
empty, bootsound in the corridors,
foreign languages in the kitchen
where the cupboard doors have been left open,
the drawers opening and falling. We attend
each eruption of gunfire, look for holes
where the rat ran.

If, here and there, we have remarked
the passing of winter, it is lamentation,
that this time of waiting might have lasted
long enough to be complete, not a world
of hurt turned to rage
and thence to war.

Last year, we were not yet foreigners,
not yet men in the kitchen, shooting rats
for fear of boys.   Not yet.   And again.

Here and there, we have taken
war for peace, and worse — for truth.

Old films, slow and sentimental, save
the blond youth looking back and losing
his grin. Everything since
has been vengeance.

Blue

The sky is nine-eleven blue
Briseis is waiting for the men to finish arguing
Achilles is pouting, as usual

All the kings' men are clichés
thinks Briseis, tucking an alphabet
carved out of stones
into her skirt

She watches cormorants and sandpipers
contemplates wading into the water
says: I will write my name on the surface
of these waves

Near the shore, the water is the color of cyanide
Farther out, darkness rises up
and snatches at the moonlight, fish-mouthed

Briseis wears a gown of indigo
a scarf stained like a robin's egg
She waits to be ransomed with gold
Her skirt grows heavy
It does not float around her waist
The water is not cold

Let me become as a rock, says Briseis
I will sink and settle, and shelter small crabs
I will crack only when burned
I will be a sign on the path, a place to rest
I will be as still and as silent as death

No one listens
The war goes on

Briseis on the shore, looks back
toward Troy and wonders what Achilles would do
in her position.
The wind fills her mouth with sand
A cloud in the shape of a horse
gallops across the horizon

Achilles, looking toward Troy, says
Let me be as a stone to my men
On me they may whet their weapons
I will be a warning, a sign and a promise
I will break bone and flesh when sharpened
I will be the marker of their graves

Briseis faces the sea, looks up
A cluster of stars forms a crab in the sky
The moon rises silver as ice
and falls in shards upon the water
At her feet, a thin line of foam

Someone skips a stone across the surf
Briseis wonders what Achilles would do
in her position

But he's not

Her skirt is heavy
The water is not cold
And the war goes redly on

Ways of Seeing

Dreaming Eden

She has lived two lives and a dream
in one body. So, say a death.
A death split her apple:
green sour, tongue cringes.
And the corpse eats bitter earth.

This great dying
in which the soldiers of millennia
fall as one to bruised soil
and the women are broken by waiting,
swells to a fruit within her.
And the grief a sickle
with which to fell the broken tree.

In her first life, she was snaked
by tempting shadows. And silent,
desire thick in a fearful mouth.
But in her death an annunciation
spoken roundly in belled words:
And you shall dream the apocryphal world.
The dream her sepulchrum,
the night a room of candles.

Unciphered tongues burn on the altar
and the dream bears the world
unworded. Her second life begins
here in the speechless dawn:
blood-wet with fisted breathing.
She is after Sarah's waiting
and bears Holofernes on her spear.
She is Jephthah's daughter raised
from sacrificial love.

From the dreaming grave, her eyes sprout
irises and bear their own messages,
cryptic as the moon's cold face.
Now over-ripe, she spits seeds
for new fruit: a pear perhaps,
or a pomegranate,
something that cannot be halved
by knowing.

Eyeless in Summer

1(:)

uneven sound of hose-spit falling,
a mercurial arc undulating
over the portulaca and the paintbrushes
in measured bloom
at the tarmac's soft black lip.

water slaps the pavement,
hisses to dryness amid the ghosts
of creosote and cut grass
and chlorine
from the neighbor's kidney-shaped pool.

always whining, the lawnmowers;
neurotic quilts of clipped green
lie fenced by white language
and a medusa head grows
from the willow's trunk.

Close your eyes.   You are blind.

2(:)

    somewhere else:
katydids rasping invisibly
in brittle grasses
stickied by blackberry juice
and dollops of cow dung,
the bees in six-week frenzies.

someone has left a red bicycle
by the river's edge,
under the arbutus tree
with its trunk peeling smoothly,
the color of cinnamon.

not ticking, the absent clock

but the bats flap haired leather
against a squatting dusk,
and remark the parting time with echoes
of shape and shifting form.

Open your eyes. It is dark out.

3(:)

    now the imagined body
goes unribbed by words
and is amphibious again, with goose flesh
bone-colored like the moon —
and interrupted by shadow.

in darkness, the trees are undressed.
old desire hangs iridescent at last
between the screen door
and the dusted rags of a moth's wing,
the final desperation of summer.

and soon, the consummate speech of the tongueless

will emerge from earthen mouths:
worms underground in the rain,
the sound of first frost before foot-steps,
and brittle leaves will fall
                from Medusa's head.

Look now. Now you are learning to see the absence
of too much light.

K, Accountant

Tenth or eleventh, depending on origin
this is the place where foreignness enters

undocumented, at the join of flesh
turned now to sound

like a hinge that opens, scraping
the ear, provoking desire with a promise

of somewhere else. And on the threshold:
a crisis of direction.

      Kufic, from Kufa;
the lettered city south of Baghdad

sounds forth its cradle's cry
and is echoed in weeping. Across

the centuries, a script of adornment is
broken. Like crystal, its shards scatter

before the drowning eyes of the scholars. Only
metaphor is adequate, another

foreignness entering the crevasse
of grief. There have been others.

      The K/T boundary
in whose lacerated relation

a whole world vanished, in heat
or in cold, perhaps under black clouds

but slowly. The largeness of animals
became useless, so that small words

and silence might find their way. Quietly
we learned to stalk our prey, to take arms

and cross ourselves, take kris and turn kiblah,
name our enemies and our flowers with one word

that also begins with K.
        Mark the word, sounding forth

across the blood-stained fields.
and pray, sing kaddish, seek the black stone

in Mecca, in Kaaba, count the ways.
It is what we do best, says Kant:

measure. Calculate the cost
of being human, and not only light

or its speed, or the distance traveled
by the thousands. To count ourselves

and find the whole wanting for having
settled, having taken what we do best

for all we do, settling our debts
in quantities of blood and bone, cut

from the living, form the breathing
the speakers of words, because

we did not understand them. This
is the disconsolate conclusion to which

reason delivers us. So says K, the name
& last sign of a struggle (ein Kampf) to be human

and not merely an accountant. You
can imagine that K, upon hearing this, runs amok

in the aviary, where the biggest birds can no longer fly
but claw the dirt and hide their heads instead.

Babel is the sound of K thrice told, a cackling
or crackling, as on the radio, when, between kHz,

the frequency of transmission is not always
attainable. Still, there is the sign of something

that might be language. A broken letter
in the desert, south of Baghdad, rustles

in the sand. We counted
the ways to kill, and in settling accounts

decapitated the world. Headless
we hope for miracles, but are afraid

they will come from afar
and speak in another tongue.

Blackest Above the Abattoir

The sky is always blackest above the abattoir
though this absence of light is itself
only the relativity of darkness.

Even on moonless nights,
acetylene clots the horizon with blue ether
where starlight might have leaked.

I pass by this place
on the way home from night — crossing
behind the soccer field
with its rhythms of leather and bone —
to where the road splits
(thrumming of toads and nocturnal
insects, a boot squashing in the mud).

Bursting in a halo of sulfur, a cigarette
makes the sky pointillist with red light and reveals:
the eye of a bull and a translucence
of pink flesh — a dilated nostril.
In the stabs of head-light, the geometry
of barbed wire cuts the sides of the bulls
like the ribbons on a Christmas gift.

They mass here, at the corner of
the field. Behind them: the prostrate building
and the sound of wet brooms sweeping.

From this place, in small trapezoids of light
that lie like tiles on the grazed earth,
the steam of blood and piss
tongues the air
and inside: the careful frame

of the virgin Mary's portrait on a distant wall.

Even from this distance, she is all eyes and blueness.
Even from this distance, she observes the young man.

Naked from the waist up, his skin shining,
he leans on his broom and from the doorway
spits tobacco juice in an arc so neat
it might have been blood.

Variorum on Emily Dickinson's Bluebird

From here	reading
across	the fold
	folds
ink	makes a wild word
	making worlds
of	a bluebird's tone
forgetting	the shrillness
forgotten	keening
the sound	on paper
the pen	drags ink
	scarifies
ink	like blood
	bleeding
in the fold	of a plume-scarred envelope
where	
a bluebird	died
	dies
like this	unremarked except
like me	excepting remark
in the sound (:).	blue scratched out
sounds	blue
in the interval	
scratching	the air/ear.

Like a skylark, on a gramophone,
interrupted by time. But blue.

Like a skylark, a gramophone
is interrupted in time not its own

not an ode.

The ode ends.   Old ends
without melancholy
in a bluebird's song.

The Astronaut in Isolation

In vaulted dark
directionless, dayless

the astronaut
thinks of flowers

grows toward green
longs for birdsong

the sound of leafstorm,
dreams of turning his face

to the sun,
        and   for a moment

in vaulted dark
directionless, dayless

feels the heat
becomes the flower.

Ways of Seeing (a Memory of Italy)

1.

The cypress tree I thought
too perfect. Translation
of stone, saltless pillar:
the landowners' sentinel
was everywhere stoic.
Its dignity: nowhere to hide
the hunter's scope.

So, we were free.

2.

What I have of that time is image:
mine and those inherited.
It's so familiar, you said.
All those paintings loved by my mother,
unvisited, except in books.
The landscape already within me.

Still, it was a surprise. The scent
of lavender in the evening.
The faithful swallows.
Scrummaging boar and
doe-eyes in the inkdark.
And in the morning, burst figs and
dewdrop on the grass.

3.

Lemon, olive, bramble and vine.
A praying mantis,
            awkward as any symbol
tumbled down the stone wall.

A leaf confessed its design.
Then another.

I did not expect to be so ravished
by green.

4.

Is there not a better word?
Than green?
Than ravished.

San Piero fishes in the grotto
with a blue net.

A small boat floats in the sky,
sails full, straining toward us
from the stone wall: still blue
in the lamplit future, looking
to Lampedusa.

5.

We too followed the roads of empire.
Amazing, we said. Poor captives
that carved these routes calligraphic
from the falling world.

It's the hottest season on record
(signs of the new times, they say)
On the horizon, an ocean mirage.

But heat is séance here.
Beneath the tar: scorched memories
of the Sahel, thirsty still
under the cypress
dreaming green.

Something Gets Planted

The Moons of Fifty

1.

There's a map of the moon
on a classroom wall, somewhere
in my childhood.

Once, I could
recite all those names:
mountains, rifles and rilles,
all those pacific seas:
Mare Cognitum or Ingenii,
Marginis and Insularum.

The only ocean, it turns out, storms
but drily.

Repeat after me.

Lacus Somniorum and Solitudinis
Temporis and Timoris.

Under Polaris
the northern explorer dreamed
water in a dead language, fled
Tranquility and Serenity (also Crises)
in search of Nectar

in the West
— or the East

depending
on how you look at it.

Southward, the dream was wish:
vapors, moisture, humors and clouds.

On the moon as on earth
everything happens twice
and then again.

2.

If I am into the second half
the night is astigmatic.
Two moons loom in the curtained room
where the table is set and waiting.
I am under a white cloth, my gown untied.

I didn't expect things to look like this
astronomer's dream.

I read science fiction,
followed the Voyager's path to Saturn,
filled a trunk with blankets, china,
woolen things   and notebooks
packed well for a long journey.

I hoped a destination would choose me.
I did not imagine a desire for return.

On winter days, I remembered
Neil Armstrong in tv snow,
delayed and dressed for other elements:
earth, air and (again) water.

Now, in the darkened room
I learn that, even on earth
the seconds hasten

and slow   at the same time.

3.

The sonographer's hands are cold.
She wears red nail polish
blue glasses, bluely lit.

Screen and lens, lens and screen:
I can almost see my eyes in hers
see myself seeing
(I could be Aldrin to her Armstrong).

I want to see what she sees,
what lurks in aqueous light.

A little more gel. *Turn toward me.*

Sound-images of the far side
flash up, recede like fish.
A cloud obscures the view.

Let's do that again. Just once more.
To be sure.

Sure. For now.
Vapors, moisture, humors and clouds.

Everything happens twice
and then again.

4.

The dream, a doubled vision:
classroom wall and computer screen,
riffled ridge and venous branch.
I used to think time was on my side.

One side and then the other:
my breasts, two moons
in tideless night.

Outside,
nine stories to earth,
autumn spurns expectation:
late blooms and second leaves,
omens of unseasonal growth.

Inside,
                the moon
                                extends its orbit,
reveals a hidden face.

5.

A pamphlet left in the waiting
room reads: *Not having children is
a factor.* Among others.

We are all anthropologists now,
treading the paths of ancestors,
searching family lines for death,
writing genealogies of risk,
fearing the future.

No one knows what the past will bring.
To be among others must be enough.

I look at the screen, follow
time's numbered trace,
attend tendril and branch, look for craters
like Tycho, that lunar pock once named a navel:
secret birthplace of mystery, or

scar of a catastrophe
that might yet recur.

Let's look again a year from now.

Everything happens twice
and then again.

Time resumes its pace
but at fifty
how far into the second half am I?

Transit of Mercury

In memory of my mother

Is there any danger
under the sign of the crab,
do the stars sear you
with cancerous destiny?

Astrologers never foretell anything.
They don't have to. If not crab,
then the heart's eruption, or some
more violent end in the collision of metal
and pavement.

Under briny rock, upturned
for science and not to disturb
the common lot, we found them,
like green platelets, hastening sideways:
the first metastasis unperceived
in metaphor.

The day was gold and blue,
salt rimmed our lips,
the pail filled with shells.

Reading Dante in St. John the Divine Cathedral

From hell above, that glow of phosphorescence
lays upon the granite like a skin — reminds us
of the Saint's unflayed form, improbably intact
despite all else. We therefore imagine this arched ceiling
as an inhalation of stone, the cavern of air its intake.
This is faith, we think. This abatement of breath is nothing
but the anticipation of something else,
and the sense of its immanence. This is faith, we think, and
we know (or think we know) that exile requires this.

We know (or think we know) that exile requires this
survival. *No sadness is greater than in misery*
to rehearse Memories of joy. So says Francesca
parting from the flock of doves whose sin, they say,
was love and the temptation of a book. Lancelot
read by two who, while reading, are joined in vision
as though in blood. To be one in viewing another
is to be as one, and thus in love, incestuous:
Love, which absolves None who are loved from loving.

Love, which absolves None who are loved from loving
is vengeful. The sin was not to suspect. The sin was
to surrender flesh to vision, to want being wanted.
John, on Patmos, writes what speaks from behind —
becomes the bell of that trumpet which is first and last —
and falls as though dead before the pages that fly
to the churches, birdlike. But birdlike is not angelic
and pages fall to books, and books to eyes which read, and reading
want, and wanting, read exile in that glow of phosphorescence

that shines from hell above and makes of love a sin.

Hudson River Rhapsody

Yesterday, when the wind came
raw from the Hudson, rasping
through unclad branches —
with only an occasional plastic bag
to snag the howl —
I thought I heard you say,

Now, go down to the river. Now
go down and rest on her great
and trembling back.

This river doesn't run. This river
sighs down the stone-pricked banks, eddies
around oil-soaked piers & paint-scabbed
tugs, styrofoam floats. It squeezes sea-bitten
gun-grey into Atlantic green, where even the gulls
moan with special melancholy
at the absence of blue.

I went down to the river, heaved over
the grey wall onto stone and scrub,
stepped over rank shit and the stains
of cheap ecstasy on soiled blankets,
walked to the water's edge amid brown
bottles. But you were quiet. No
still small voice called out,
asking for obedience. So
I stayed.

Now you.
Go down to the water's edge.
Say I am here.

A taste of salt
    and sea, dark deep down.
Trembling. Your back. Me a river, running
and sighing. A seagull doesn't moan.
I do. You do. Me a river.
And the Hudson still grey, raw and going
elsewhere.

If you said go now, down would be all.

Latenight, Called by You

Latelatenight
called by you   and
moonlight   the sound of no bird
and branchbreak beneath
the foot the code grown restless

Memory gives up
what starlight won't forget
how   despite the sending
the message   grown restless
I,   called late by you

Beneath the bird, the branch
breaks code and wrestles
starlight from the sky,
the moon gives you up
late, and I, restless   call.

Sappho's Foot

for Yvette

Think of Sappho, her strange foot. The foot [
    ] is
          ] everything. To walk, stand [
    Come to me.   [ ] Footfalls:
    Ciphers

of arrivals and departures, quiet exits from
the bedroom where the sheets cool too quickly, or
the tender approach when night has overwhelmed
want and waiting is sleep. Say only
    goodnight.

I think of you this way: thin rind of callous
cupping the heel, or a new moon, silver &
sharp in winter sky, or (yet again) black earth
    under the gardener's finger nail.
    To be

so   so   close   (if whispered, it would be enough).
and still [
    ] to fear losing
    as by forgetting, or (perhaps?) some
    ruin

when the interval would not imply return but
a vanishing, like her [   ]
words missed   perhaps a voice
    but not silent, rather invisible
    What

comes with age   that need   to be needed
and to know that one will not fail, not stumble

when everything depends on quickness — no blanks
          ...] no forgotten numbers
          the telephone

unmenacing. To walk steadily and say
and believe in saying — with the gods — we still
have time and   ] love
          after: promise you, promise me:
          to survive

Now, other things come to mind: me behind you,
heat, a smoothness [ ]   your back
cupped by me   as by a moon, or a callous.
          My breast flat, your arm reaching
          back

] ear,

          eye
          hand and foot   you
          Come to me.   [ ]   dreaming as if
          agelessly.

Something Gets Planted

*Something gets planted in you when you have a garden
that makes you care for every living thing.*
—Gunda Ingeborg Lien, née Svensen, age 106

Something gets planted

> The last lesson, precipient sermon
> in the language of cold-weather perennials :
>
> sovereign rhubarb, loyal potato and
> potted chrysanthemum, because : they last.
>
> At a certain point, time past and time
> present are one. The future
> evanesces.
>
> She notices the
> unticking clock the
> fixed hand, waiting for :
>
> accidental correctness, the harvest of hours.
> *Can you fix it*, she asks?

When you have a garden

> Hands like shovels, they said :
> all the held things, the kneaded things
>
> the struck and broken things
> (before the burial of imagined repair)
>
> have left their mark in the
> cupped shape, uncalloused now,

flesh like onion skin
onion : the
manumission
of sorrow.

When you have a garden

Time past and time present
are one. The nurse forms her words

theatrically, shows them on her lips
to the deaf eye, rheumred and bluestill.

On the windowsill
the robin's blue eggs are breaking their code :

every April is now.
                    Now, now
says the nurse, time for
bed.

Unfurl the peashoot dream.
Sometimes, I cannot find my way back.

Something gets planted

She inhales ancient
apples perfuming
the firstlight

recalls the bitter consolations of winter :
rutabaga and parsnip,

tin-cup coffee and tumid
pumpkin. The sky discloses
its prophecy of rain

and she is grateful.   Now, amid the
slow decay her body grows machinic :

rasp and sigh, the
intake of air a storm in
her throat.

For every living thing

From leafrot and
earthlust, the
conjugation of corpses

renews the breakage between
generations. *Keep learning*, she
says.

*I have seen a lot, but not
everything*. At a certain point, time
past and time

present are one. All tense vanishes.
A friend says, 'The dead continue to communicate;

we have only to decipher their
messages.' I dream of ash in my ears.

Every living thing

No one knows how difficult, how
painful the entry into growing :

unheard tearing and breach of
pod, the surface giving way to
pressing sky

to wounding nurturing light : all
being toward the abandonment of
now,

to going forward, to keeping going.
She knows : the first tense to vanish is conditional.

If I heard her call to me, she would say
Come. And I would answer : not now.

Notes and Acknowledgments

This book is dedicated to Yvette, from whom I have learned what poetry can teach. It is also indebted to the friendship and inspiring examples of Ingrid de Kok and Antjie Krog. Additional thanks are offered to the two readers who reviewed the manuscript for Fordham, Ed Pavlić and John Weir, and to Richard Morrison, whose editorial guidance and support of this volume has earned him my most profound gratitude.

All fragments that form "If in a Tomb" are drawn from the letters of Ethel and Julius Rosenberg. The original letters were published as *Death House Letters of Ethel and Julius Rosenberg* in 1953 (New York: Jero) prior to the Rosenbergs's execution. The volume is prefaced by a poem by Ethel Rosenberg, titled "If We Die." It is written for her two sons, Michael and Robert.

"Sappho's Foot" appeared in the *Capilano Review,* ed. Jenny Penberthy, vol. 2, no. 49 (Spring 2006): 97–99.

"Blackest Above the Abattoir: A Memoir of Belize" and "Letters to the Front in a Time of AIDS" originally appeared in *Carapace 37,* ed. Ingrid de Kok, June 2002, 10–13.

"Here and There" was first published in *Literary Imagination* 8, no. 3 (2006): 528.

"The Astronaut in Isolation" appeared in the *Daily Maverick,* April 30, 2020.

"Huntsville, TX," first appeared as "Current," in *Ideas and Futures,* April 2021.

Rosalind Morris, Professor of Anthropology at Columbia University, is a prolific writer and scholar. Her recent books include *Unstable Ground: The Lives, Deaths, and Afterlives of Gold in South Africa* and *Accounts and Drawings from Underground*, co-created with William Kentridge. Recognized with Rockefeller and Guggenheim fellowships, a Berlin Prize, and residencies at prestigious institutions, as well as film festival prizes, Morris's academic and creative works traverse disciplinary boundaries with artfulness, courage, and precision. Visit www.rosalindcmorris.com for more.

O₁ /₄

∫